Critter's Choice

Cherrie Adams

Illustrations: Lucinda Gregory

First published by Busybird Publishing 2020

Copyright text © 2020 Cherrie Adams

Copyright illustrations © 2020 Lucinda Gregory

978-1-922465-10-8 (paperback)

This work is copyright. Apart from any use permitted under the *Copyright Act 1968*, no part of this publication may be reproduced, stored in a retrieval system or transmitted in any form or by any means, electronic, mechanical, photocopying, recording or otherwise, without the prior written permission of Cherrie Adams.

Cover Image: Lucinda Gregory

Layout and typesetting: Busybird Publishing

Illustrations: Lucinda Gregory

Busybird Publishing
2/118 Para Road
Montmorency, Victoria
Australia 3094

Dedicated to those who knew and loved Critter Adams and for all those who ache with the loss of a loved one. May this story offer you some comfort.

PART 1

Materna

In a Universe above the above, beyond the beyond and further than the furthest knowing, resides a heavenly body that holds the beginnings of all Life. It sits in the space past the barely there blue sky, into the silky ink of midnight hue, and onto sightless darkness. Beyond this is where the colours of the Universe end and the colours of Eternity bestow their gentle light. This heavenly body has existed before everything, spinning in a timeless continuum.

This world of luminosity is called Ørtus.

To know of its existence is to have begun there, to remember its existence is to have returned there. All life comes from this sacred place and eventually journeys to every part of this Universe.

Ørtus is the beginning for all, and the return for a chosen few.

I am Materna, the Guardian of Ørtus and the Mother Eternal. My love is unconditional and infinite.

The galaxies that swirl in my all-seeing eyes have witnessed the birth of worlds so beautiful that I have bowed my head in reverence. I have observed the death of stars and constellations and the formation of unending galaxies, engaged with beings of unimagined form and intelligence that inhabit this vast magnificence. All are precious. I am a multi-dimensional shifter; time and distance are not relevant to me. I am everywhere, always watching my charges.

Those charges are the Evos of Ørtus.

Evos are the beginnings of all things. From them everything else evolves. They are beings of innocence who all start as the same entities on Ørtus. Their purpose is to learn and study and eventually be assigned a destination, anywhere in this Universe. Whilst I am the Guardian of Ørtus and the Evos, the task of attending to their complex learning in preparation for their destinations, is managed by the Wise Ones. These beings hold the collective wisdom of all species in this Universe, from the beginning of everything.

The Wise Ones are all-knowing and once an Evo has been assessed for suitability to a destination, recommendations are made to the Record Keeper who is the custodian of the Sacred Records. Within the pages of the Sacred Record Books are the destination numbers and tasks for all Evos leaving Ørtus. The role of Record Keeper has been passed down reverentially. It is a precise and immensely important job. Destination suitability, and astrological compatibility are vital to the success of the Evo's placement.

Once an Evo has been allocated a destination number, they are assigned that number and transported to their destination, taking on the form of the inhabitants of that place.

Some are sent to distant celestial bodies to be great discoverers, or keepers of ancient texts. Others may become the lifeform for an emerging colony. No task is greater or lesser in this cosmic transfer.

There is one group of Evos, however, who are selected because of their exceptional qualities.

These Evos display an adaptable attitude and an aptitude for problem solving, which assists them to navigate their sometimes difficult tasks on a planet called Earth. It lies in a spiral galaxy called the Milky Way. A speck in an ever unfolding and expanding Universe.

The inhabitants of this destination are Humans. They are the only beings in the Universe to experience the biggest challenge of all, emotions. Humans have a finite lifespan, so the Record Keeper ensures that any of my Evos that are sent there are given a specific Life's Mission to achieve, and an exit date to return. Should they not have completed their Life's Mission by their allocated exit date, they will return to Ørtus and be sent back to Earth as many times as necessary. Once their Life's Mission has been completed, they return to Ørtus permanently.

Upon return to Ørtus, the Evos have two roles. They are mentors to the new and emerging Evos and also act as guides and, eventually, exit messengers for their Earth families when their lives are due to finish. This is the returning Evos' most important role.

***

The Record Keeper was nearing the end of his custodianship and, once completed, he would be free to live on Ørtus without any further responsibility to the Sacred Records. He had completed all tasks with perfection and soon it would be time to pass the Sacred Record Books to another.

This is how it is meant to be. Occasionally, however, an Evo causes a ripple in the system and that comes with uncertain consequences.

One of the Evos was so engrossed in watching a game of Skyball that he had not noticed me gliding towards him. The shimmer of my gown, reflecting starlight and cosmic colours, eventually caught his attention.

'Isn't it time for you to be in class?' I asked.

I peered at the disgruntled face before me and smiled. I had observed this particular one before. Always wanting to rush through lessons, then head off to a game of Skyball or some other energetic pursuit. I know a rule bender, a cloud rider, or a bored Evo when I see one.

'I was going, but I ...' The unfinished sentence hung in the luminous glow, like a pair of drying spirit-wings.

'Yes?'

'Well, I am just bored!'

Ah, yes. True to form. The restless ones are easily bored with their lessons, always wanting to be doing something else!

'I want to go down there. I want to be a human boy.'

A long slender finger was pointing in the direction of a place far, far away. Beyond the clouds, through the darkness and into the light, where I knew that a small blue-green planet sat proudly in the infinite vastness that enveloped it.

EARTH.

The most challenging, yet the most loving of all the destinations.

I folded my arms into my gossamer-light robe and contemplated how many times over multiple millennia I had heard this from a restless Evo. It is always the ones who are impatient and want things to happen NOW! They are sometimes reckless. They often have the greatest potential for feelings and that is the problem. If they are assigned to the blue-green planet, to be humans, their lessons are often very difficult.

Humans not only have to navigate intelligence and emotions, but they are also endowed with the extra complication of choice. Every lesson and life experience offers a choice. It is not always obvious and they have to see that for themselves. Added to this is that every choice comes with a consequence for which the humans are responsible. Earth is a very tough assignment, and yet so very rewarding. But being human takes courage!

I gazed down at the upturned face staring at me. Exuberance and restlessness, combined with all that being human entailed, may be too challenging for this one. Still, it is not I who wrote the Sacred Record Books, and only the Record Keeper would have that information for this one!

'Why are you in such a rush? You have more to learn before the Wise One finishes your studies and suggests where you will be most suited, and then the Record Keeper will assign you a destination. Be patient. Your turn will come once you are properly prepared. Now, off you go to your classes and when the time is right I will summon you to the Record Keeper for further instruction.'

The Evo shrugged and turned away dejectedly, muttering. I caught the words as he drifted past me, 'Somehow I will get to Earth. I just know I will.'

I watched as the Restless Evo dashed away. There had been many like this one of course, but eventually they all embraced their new destinations. I had no doubt this one would be okay too. The Restless Evo still had work to do and would not be going any time soon.

The timelessness of Ørtus meandered along. As Evos completed their studies, they were assigned and sent to their destinations. Those who were still learning were assembled in their small groups, waiting for the instruction for the lessons to begin. When the Wise One arrived, he cast his eyes over the small groups congregated before him and was about to welcome them, when he noticed one was missing. The assembled Evos looked at one another wondering why the Wise One was just standing still, gazing out at the unending expanse of space that surrounded Ørtus.

A peculiar look came over the Wise One's face. Not anger, because that was not possible on Ørtus. But annoyance was and, yes, he definitely looked annoyed!

His gaze rested on a scene beyond the learning place where a young Evo was sitting and speaking animatedly to a newly returned Evo who had completed his time on Earth. This did not surprise the Wise One. This particular Evo, the restless one, was always seeking out returned Evos and hanging onto every word about their mission and experiences.

The Wise One had spoken to this Evo before about missing class and now his patience was exhausted. He would speak to Materna and suggest that this one be assigned in the next group. He was not quite ready, but ready enough for a destination of solitude and reflection.

***

The Record Keeper and the Wise One were sitting in the Grand Reading Chamber. They were surrounded with the words of the Ancients and all the knowledge in the Universe. It was a sacred and revered space.

'That just leaves this one,' said the Record Keeper, displaying an image of the Restless Evo.

'Hmmmm', was the only response from the Wise One.

'Are you satisfied that he has sufficient learning to be assigned a destination?' asked the Record Keeper.

There was a long pause before the Wise One replied. Thoughts of the time spent with this Evo came flooding back. This Evo had actually completed his work sufficiently well to go into this group's destination discussions. In spite of his lack of focus at times, and his ability to be easily distracted, he had managed to impress the Wise One and the Record Keeper with his will. It seemed to drive his restlessness and his discontent. Still, his energy vibrated highly and, when channelled properly, would be an asset to the Restless Evo at the destination he was about to be assigned.

'So?' the Record Keeper queried, 'Do you have a shortlist of recommendations?'

'No, not a short list, just one option,' replied the Wise One. 'I have decided that this one needs discipline and structure to harness that will and restlessness. So I have recommended Destination 16.'

'Oh,' the Record Keeper replied. 'That comes as a bit of a surprise. I thought that will and determination might be suited to a new and emerging colony that needs energy and an adventurous spirit, perhaps 26, or even 14?'

They both fell silent.

The Record Keeper then added, 'Destination 16 is a very solitary assignment and one that requires much self-regulation. Of course I know that you have thought on this, but how do you think he will manage without direction?'

'THAT is the point,' the Wise One replied. 'This one has the potential for greatness, but without self-regulation, there will only be chaos. Let's watch this one and when he has proven himself, might we not consider a reassignment?'

'That is most irregular,' said the Record Keeper. 'The Sacred Record Books are very specific about destination assignment. I don't know that there has ever been a reassignment. No, I cannot agree to this. I will look at all three destinations and study the astrological compatibility for him and let you know my decision, as directed by the Sacred Record Books.'

The Wise One nodded. His task was to instruct and recommend, not to make the final decision.

The Record Keeper collected all the other Evos' charts before him and placed the Restless Evo's on the top. 'I will consult the astrology for each of these other Evos and if all is well, will arrange their destination robes.'

He then tapped the Restless Evo's chart and said, 'Whatever the destination for this one, I agree he needs to focus his energy. Once I have decided, I will arrange for him to leave in the next exodus.'

As he was leaving, Materna appeared in the doorway. She saw the papers cradled in the crook of his arms.

'Is the next group assigned?'

'Yes,' the Wise One and the Record Keeper replied in unison.

'I was just about to complete their astrological charts and then, if all is in accordance with the Ancient Records, I will advise you so that you can prepare the Evos to come to me,' said the Record Keeper.

Materna wanted to ask about the Restless Evo, but knew that the decisions were final. She would know soon enough what had been determined for this Evo.

With their lessons finished for the day, many Evos were busy playing or absorbed in a game of Skyball. The competition was fierce and none was more competitive than the Restless Evo who had joined a group of Evos who had recently received their destination robes. Their numbers glowed brightly in the Ørtus light and the Restless Evo scanned their numbers, looking for any of the coveted Earth destination numbers. There were a couple in this group who had been allocated Earth, so he was elated that maybe HE might be too!

The game they were playing was engrossing. A newly assigned Evo, proudly wearing his Ø10 robe, dropped the skyball skilfully onto his foot, and launched it above the heads of the opposing team, where his good friend, Ø15, was ready to catch it and run to the scoring circle. As the skyball arched itself high into the air, the Restless Evo, who was on the opposing team, prepared to intercept it and run like the wind to the scoring position. This would win them the game. As the Restless Evo took his first step, ready to fly high to take the ball, Materna appeared, directly in the path of the ball!

'MOOOOOVE!' came a cry.

The other Evos froze mid-game. Had someone actually shouted at Materna?

She stood calm and serene. Not a sound from her lips.

The skyball fell to the ground and rolled to a standstill. No one and nothing moved.

There was a pause while all of the Evos waited for her response, but Materna just smiled and glided towards them, stopping in front of the restless one.

'I have great news. You have been assigned your destination. It is time for you to go to the Record Keeper, who will get all the necessary things in order. Listen carefully. It's very important that you pay attention,' she said.

'Great, I have a destination. I hope it's Earth. That's my choice. It looks so beautiful,' said the Restless Evo.

'You know that you don't get to choose,' Materna said. 'Hurry along now. The Record Keeper has all your instructions. You are ready for this, but remember, listen carefully to everything he tells you.'

As Materna stretched out her hand to hold the hand of the one before her, a shot of energy rushed through her body. She gasped. This one's energy was strong!

The Record Keeper was waiting at his magnificently crafted crystal table for the next Evo to receive their destination number. He knew that some had to be encouraged to go, but as he looked over the top of his eye enhancers, he saw one racing towards him, barefooted, robe flying and a space-dust-smudged face that carried an enormous grin.

My Goodness, this one is keen! mused the Record Keeper.

The Evo asked, 'Earth, am I going to Earth?'

The Record Keeper didn't answer, just looked at his ancient Sacred Record Book and at the chapter titled: *Destination Numbers and their Life's Mission*, then handed the Evo a soft fabric pouch with mystical symbols emblazoned on the outside. The symbols glowed with light energy that infused the contents.

'Here is your new robe with your destination number on it. Please wear it until your departure in a few days. This robe represents your destination and will begin to prepare you for the life you will soon be living. It may feel strange at first, but trust me; you will soon feel the essence of your destination.

'Now let me see. Oh here it is. You have been allocated Destination 16.' As the Evo donned the new numbered robe, the Record Keeper read from his sacred book.

'Ah, no, you are NOT going to Earth, but to a similar planet in Constellation Phoenix. Planet 2763497-10*.'

The Restless Evo, now Ø16, was disappointed. The kindly Record Keeper saw this and added, 'You will be happy there. Your time will be filled with much learning. You will live a calm and gentle life, pursuing study and quiet contemplation. This will ease your restless self. There are other Evos that you know assigned there too. You will not be alone.'

Ø16 tilted his head, jutting out his determined chin and lifted his eyes to stare at the Record Keeper.

'But I want adventure! Please can't I go to Earth? I have heard such wonderful stories!'

The Record Keeper shook his head, his long hair and beard swaying from side to side in silver unison. 'It is fixed. Your studies, your aptitude and temperament, as well as the astrological readings, all suggest this is your most beneficial destination. This might well be your first lesson, to NOT get your own way! You cannot choose this next life. Your job is to make the most of it. Because you have not been assigned Planet Earth, you will not return to Ørtus. Your Life's Mission will start and finish on Planet 2763497-10*. It is good work and very satisfying. Quiet and calming.'

The newly numbered Evo was listening, but not really hearing. Ø16 was actually thinking about how unfair it all seemed. It was his life to navigate after all. Surely that meant he could make the choices? Ø16 was about to argue, when something caused a distraction. The Skyball game had resumed and one of the other Evos, Ø22, was now playing. From the corner of his eye, Ø16 saw Ø22 take a long run up to take a shot at the ball. As his foot connected, the skyball skewed off to one side and was heading, at speed, right for the Record Keeper's head!

Ø16's reflexes kicked in immediately. Lunging forward and grabbing the Record Keeper, they fell to the ground, and then, in a spectacular leap, Ø16 grabbed the skyball in both hands, passed it off to a nearby player, before twisting into a perfectly executed somersault. Except it wasn't so perfect! On the way down an outstretched hand knocked the edge of the table and all the Record Keeper's books and charts scattered. A page of the Record Book was ripped and cosmic ink splattered the rest.

In a moment that would become life changing, the **6** on Ø16's new robe became loose during the somersault and rearranged itself into a **9**!

The Record Keeper was dazed. The tumble had disoriented him. He brushed cosmic cloud strands from his tunic and from his eyes. He looked up, only to see a blurry figure striding towards him. His eye enhancers where nowhere to be found, and his head was muddled. He squinted and vaguely made out the shape of an Evo strolling towards him.

'Did you see that? What a screamer!'

The Record Keeper wasn't thinking about Skyball, he was peering at the number on the robe coming towards him. Ø**19**. Was this one of the ones going today? He couldn't remember.

He looked at his record book crumpled and stained on the ground, and exclaimed, 'Oh dear!'

Gazing with blurry vision at the book, he thumbed through the pages. When and where had Ø**19** been allocated?

'I'm sorry,' the Restless Evo began, 'Let me help you.'

But the Record Keeper waved the Evo away dismissively, as he squinted his eyes tightly to peer at the crumpled pages in his book. To his horror, he saw that Ø**19** was in fact supposed to be entering Planet Earth in exactly 58 minutes. To miss this deadline was to disrupt the order of Ørtus.

'Hurry, hurry!' he shouted at the confused Ø16 who had not noticed that his number had slipped.

'Who me?' Ø16 asked.

'Yes, yes, yes Ø19, there is NO time to lose. It's your turn to go NOW! Hurry! You don't want to miss the departure window to Planet Earth.'

The confused Evo stood still and tried to speak, 'B, b, but...'

'No time to talk, just GO! NOW!' said the Record Keeper.

'Run to the edge of the platform, the Celestial Slide is ready and waiting.'

The Record Keeper, through strained eyes, peered at his journal. 'Yes, this is right,' he read from the book:

Destination 19
Entry to Planet Earth: 25091989 at 1109
Departure from Planet Earth: 19...?
Life's Mission ...?

Oh dear, the rest of the page had been ripped and stained in the tumble. He was not going to be able to tell **Ø19** his return date to Ørtus, or his assigned Life's Mission.

Oh dear!

He wanted to call out to the Evo, that there was information missing and that he would have to watch for signs from Materna, but at that precise moment, the confused Evo, was being bundled by two large Feather Spirits, the celestial attendants, towards the Celestial Slide into **Ø19's** slot!

'Wait a minute. It's a mis—'

Then the Evo stopped.

Did the Record Keeper say **19**? That was one of the Earth numbers! Earth was what he wanted, even if it was a mistake. Wow, this was perfect! There was no time to think on it further as the two Celestial Slide attendants had grabbed one of his arms each and were guiding him towards a magnificent crystal chute. They smiled at one another and said, as one, 'It's okay, everyone is nervous, but it is a great ride and when you enter Earth, you will not remember a thing!'

They popped him onto a golden chair, pulled down the crystal dome, and with no more ceremony than that, PUSHED.

The Evo was away! Sliding effortlessly on a gold and silver slide that was studded with crystals and gems from far off galaxies. It was magnificent and as it wound its way out of the cosmic clouds and plunged into a magnificently lit sky, the newly despatched Evo sat back and looked in wonder at the panorama. Through the crystal dome roof, he saw stars and planets, strange beings and a nearby spacecraft of peculiar design and materials. Other Celestial Slides were weaving and stretching across the vastness to other unknown destinations and galaxies.

The ride was exhilarating. It was thrilling. It was description defying. It was terrifying!

After a time a small blue-green planet came into view. It was beautiful and it was going to be home for ... *Wait a minute! The Record Keeper did not give me my exit plan and date! Or my Life's Mission! How will I know when my living time is over? How will I know how to leave? And what is it I am supposed to learn on Planet Earth?*

Lost in these fearful thoughts, Materna's voice reverberated around the Crystal Dome.

'You will not remember Ørtus when you are away from here, not at least until your exit day is approaching. Trust that I will be watching and guiding you. Everything you need to know is deep within your heart. Your heart is the key to your Life's Mission. Trust your heart.'

The end of the Celestial Slide raced towards him, and he knew he was about to be born as a human.

'Oh well,' he said into the silence, 'there's nothing left to do but, *Get this thing done!*'

A moment later, exactly 58 earth minutes after leaving his heavenly home, Ø16 who was now Ø19, made a swift and spectacular entrance into the place called Earth.

Meanwhile…

'Did our Evo get any information about the complexities of going to Earth? And WHERE on Earth is he?' asked Materna.

'Well, no,' the Record Keeper replied. 'There was a mishap and well, the end result is that Ø16, who I thought was **Ø19**, has now been despatched to EARTH, instead of his intended destination as written in the Sacred Record Book. Let me check where on Earth. Oh yes, here it is, he …'

'Yes?'

'Now that he is **Ø19** he will have that life. He has been born into a family of a mother and father and two older brothers in …' he paused. 'Broken Hill NSW, in Australia.'

They peered down into the world and saw the mining town with its red desert and large blue sky. They saw the rich minerals beneath the surface of the land, the headframes and the expanses of wide sunburnt land. They saw a family gathered around smiling and cuddling their new son and baby brother.

'I didn't get to instruct him on his Life's Mission OR when and how to exit. Oh dear!'

'What is **Ø19's** Life's Mission?' asked Materna.

As the Record Keeper opened the Sacred Record Book, Materna saw the damaged page where the exit date and the Life's Mission were indecipherable to the Record Keeper's eyes.

She peered at the page with her galaxy-filled eyes and smiled. She knew what they were. The Record Keeper listened while she told him.

'Are you going to tell him while he is on the Celestial Slide?' the Record Keeper asked.

Materna pondered on this. What is best for this particular one? Now that he will be a human boy, she wondered if it was not best for him to face his challenges and learn his lessons using all the strength and determination that he has shown. Life may be hard for him, emotionally, but he will have plenty of support and of course, she would be watching him with keen interest.

'No,' she replied, 'I have a good feeling about this one. There is strength, and a stubborn yet independent streak. I think this will serve him well in his mortal life. Let us watch over him and see how he navigates his way. It seems he got his wish. An Earth Boy!'

Together they watched the tableau playing out in that historic mining town.

They saw the family who were instantly besotted with their new son and brother and heard the name Christopher, then Critter.

'Hmm,' she mused. 'Critter by name and perhaps by nature. We will watch, wait and see!'

***

Ø19 was now a human boy.

The entry into his new life had been rapid and in that moment of becoming human he gasped with the enormity of birth. The experience of the first beat of a heart was so profound that it was beyond anything he had ever experienced.

He could not identify it, only that he was overcome with a feeling that he could not describe. He did not have the experience or language yet. That would come with time. For now, he felt the warmth of liquid pumping around this new form, his body. He could hear a beat vibrating from a heart that was placed in the centre of his chest. This body was complicated, perfectly made and he had no idea yet of its capabilities, or its frailties. He only knew for sure that being human was full of what Materna had called feelings and emotions and he wanted to experience them all!

Space, by Critter, age 6

PART 2

Critter

18th November, 2015

A sigh escapes from my mouth, long and exhausted. I have been watching the slash of a November Adelaide sky that I can glimpse, if I sit up high against my pillows. Since I have been here I have seen ten (or is it nine?) sunrises and I imagine the sunsets that fall on the other side of the building each night. I think of it as moving art. My sigh is not from a lack of appreciation for the free art show in the a.m. and the imagined one in the p.m., but for the colourless boredom that stretches between my light shows.

I once saw a movie called *Groundhog Day*. The main character lived the same day, every day, for a week or more. It was pretty funny to watch, but as I am now experiencing my own Groundhog Day, it's somehow less amusing.

I am in hospital.

There is a bandage around my head and the leads and tubes attached to me are connected to various monitors that flash and beep and record my information. I am in a hospital gown and my feet are clad in bright orange socks, with white risen dots. I think they're so I don't slip when I get up to walk, but so far I have been bed bound since my surgery. I have an awful headache and feel disconnected from this reality.

My single room is comfortable and practical. When they brought me down from ICU in the early hours of this morning, I was actually happy to be back in my own room. I figured if they had transferred me from ICU already, then things must be positive. Maybe I will get to go home soon. Hospital is definitely not where I want to be.

The days are long and the nights even longer. I am grateful when friends and family come to visit. During that time I can pretend, and almost believe, that I am just a twenty-six-year-old guy and chillin'. It's harder though when my parents visit. They get that anxious look in their eyes and try too hard to be cheery, or they just talk about the practical stuff like forms to be completed and appointments to make and medication to monitor.

They DO Doing. I'm not being ungrateful, but I truly can't even think about all that crap. I just want my life back. I just want everything to be how it was eleven months ago.

'Hi Honey.'

It's my mum. She is pushing open the door to my room with her foot whilst balancing a fruit smoothie, a cappuccino, a bag of clean clothes and her *I am cheery* smile.

'Hi, Mum,' I reply.

'How are you feeling today, Darling?' she asks.

'Not great. Headaches and not much sleep. I've asked for some pain relief, but no one has come back yet.'

'I'll go and find someone, and get it sorted,' she announces. She looks relieved that she can DO something for me.

I sip my smoothie while I wait for her return and daydream that later today my wonderful surgeon will visit with her wide smile and look at me with her kind dark eyes and say:

'Well Chris, things are looking fabulous. You are doing so well, I think that we can arrange for you to go home in forty-eight hours.'

It's a trick I do. You know, like, you think of the thing that is most likely NOT to happen and you trick yourself into believing that it will. On occasions it has worked a treat. I am, however, not sure that even my active imagination can stretch that far! I am lost in that thought when the door to my room swings open with force, and Mum bursts through.

'Okay,' she says breathlessly, 'someone will be here soon to give you some pain meds.'

'Ta Mum. I hope you didn't make a fuss, they are pretty short staffed and busy in this ward.'

'No,' she replies, way too quickly. 'I just made sure it would happen.'

Hmmm.

I close my eyes and let the pain wash over me. It is unrelenting, yet familiar. It has been my companion on and off for many months now. It is the messenger that speaks of unwellness and life changes. It is not welcomed.

I hear the door open again and the clanging of a metal trolley. I open my eyes to see Sam standing there. He is my nurse in this ward and he is a champion bloke. He has dreadlocks tied back in a band, an earring and a nose piercing. He wears a red string on his wrist and a crystal around his neck. He is a pretty cool guy. The last time I was in here, about a month ago, he came in at the end of his shift with a family-size meatlover's pizza and two cans of coke. We pigged out on the pizza and watched the cricket together. Champion bloke. He talks to me like a regular guy. He says I should try meditation and maybe get into yoga and, if I want to try it once I am discharged, he will pick me up and take me to the place he goes. He reckons it will help settle my 'monkey mind'. That's what he calls it. You know, that incessant chatter that just won't bugger off. Mum and Dad suggested it too, but somehow hearing it from a guy more my age makes more sense to me. I think I might try it, once I am discharged.

'Hi, mate,' he says, while picking something up from the trolley.

'I hear you are running a bit rough this morning.' He casts a cautious look in my mum's direction. She is busy studying her coffee; a slight smirk sits on her orange lip-sticked mouth.

'Yeah, Sam,' I reply. 'I'm feeling bloody ordinary.'

'Let's see what we can do about that.'

'I will pop in to the guest lounge for a bit,' says Mum, 'and give Dad a call.'

Sam checks my temperature (normal), blood pressure (a bit low), checks my IV and asks a few questions. He shines a light into my eyes and writes something on my chart. Then, finally, he picks up the syringe and administers some pain relief.

'It should kick in pretty soon,' he says. 'I will come back in an hour or so to check on you, buddy.'

I lie back on the pillows and think about my latest surgery. Another exploration followed by a few anxious days while we wait for the latest results. I feel so angry. It's so bloody exhausting trying to keep positive when the statistics tell a different story. Still, they are just statistics but I am not. I am Critter! I like to do things MY way.

Mum is back. 'Dad sends his love and hopes you will be feeling better soon. He will be home on the weekend. Maybe you will be out of here by then too!' Her smile looks tight. Forced, fake, but I know she is trying to keep positive too.

I can feel the pain relief washing over my aching head, like a waterfall of oblivion.

My eyes flutter. Shutting, opening, shutting again.

'Sorry, Mum I don't feel like talking. I think I will be able to sleep now.'

'Of course love. I will sit for a bit until you nod off.'

It's quiet. Just the hum of the monitors and the sounds outside my room of a busy ward. I can feel myself succumbing to sleep, and then it happens! That mind chatter interrupts my longed-for slumber. I begin to think of all the things that I still want to do. Will I get the chance? Will I have the time? I feel my anxiety rising.

'Mum!' I call out.

She leaps up from the chair, startled by my voice.

'Are you okay, do you want me to buzz Sam?'

'No,' I say. My voice sounds strange to me. A bit slurred. 'I was just thinking about all the things I still want to do and instead I'm stuck in this place. It's so fucked up. I haven't got time to waste. What if the results are crap? What if it's bad news?'

I can hear the words coming from my mouth and want them to stop. I want to stay optimistic and strong. But I'm frightened.

She is looking at me with her sad eyes.

'Critter, when you began this journey you told us to keep positive and to keep doing life as normal. You said that's what you wanted. So, why not write down all the things you want to do when you're feeling better. It can be your wish list.'

'You mean Bucket List,' I snap back. Words weighted with venom.

'Things to do before I die.'

A resounding silence balances between us, a tightrope walker over the Grand Canyon.

I have said them. The unspoken, the taboo words.

She looks at me, but says nothing, just reaches into her bag and pulls out a pen and a notebook. She opens the first page and writes something, then closes it and puts them on the bedside cabinet.

'You need to rest,' she says.

She leans over and places her lips on my forehead, resting there for a moment, hand on my chest. I feel her pain, she feels mine.

'I think Jen and dear Archie are coming in later, and Ellie too. Try to sleep now darling.'

I want to say sorry, or something, but the words won't come. Instead I nod and say, 'Thanks for coming in Mum. See you later.' And then add, 'Love you, bye.'

I am determined to sleep, but my monkey mind is full on chattering. The notebook and pen are lying on the bedside cabinet where Mum had left them. I look at them. What had she written?

As I open the cover I see her writing:

Sweetheart,

Make your plans fearlessly; be as adventurous as you wish. It's YOUR life … go for it!

Love you

Mum   xxxx

I reach for the notebook and with the pen between my teeth, I ask myself:

What are the things I still want, or maybe, need to do?

So the statistics are poor for me, long term. But who decides that? Surely I have some say. It's MY life after all.

As I think those words, they sound strangely familiar to me, from a long forgotten memory.

Before I know it, my thoughts are coming thick and fast and words are flying across the page. Now that I have started, I am feeling really excited about the possibility of achieving some of these plans.

'Maybe it will ALL come true,' I say out loud, into my empty room.

The sound of the monitor acts like a lullaby. I am drifting away. Sleep, blessed sleep at last.

Muffled voices. I wrench myself from my sleep cave and focus my eyes. I am happy to see Jen and my three-year-old nephew, Archie. They flew down from Brisbane a few days ago. Jen is married to my brother Matty and she came to see me in ICU the night of my surgery. It was pretty surreal, because Jen is six months pregnant with their second baby, another boy. I felt him kick when she leant over the railing around my bed to kiss me. I can't explain how amazing that felt. I remember the kind look in her eyes when she saw my surprise, and she just let me rest my hand on her belly. Jen is quiet like that. Just gentle and calm and knows how to read a situation. She smiled and saw that I was feeling an incredible connection with this baby. Like I already knew him. It stirred a memory of something, fleeting, of another world, ethereal, and then it was gone. Must be the post-operative anaesthetic, I decide. I can't wait to meet nephew number two!

I see Mum is back and Ellie is with her. She hands me a berry smoothie and a cheerful smile. Ellie is a kind soul with a loving heart and has been a great support to us all. She beams as she tells me that she has just sat her final Uni exam. I know she will do just fine. I see the relief written all over her face.

I remember that feeling!

I finished four years of uni to get my Bachelor of Business in Marketing. I don't know why I chose that course, it's not like I enjoyed it! But I have a framed degree now that Mum insisted went up on my bedroom wall. My graduation was in April, a few months ago and I really didn't want to go. But I reckon it was more for Mum and Dad and as Hannah, my girlfriend, said, 'You will regret it when you look back later in life that you didn't go and get your cap and gown, Chrissy.'

I went, but felt uncomfortable. I remember waiting on the side of the stage to be called forward and feeling so bloody nervous because I couldn't see properly from my left eye, (courtesy of my surgery) and was worried that I might trip and fall over, but I managed to get through it and I guess I feel proud now that I did it, though I hate the photos. I was bald from the chemo and radiation and bloated from the steroids. Later that day, I had another seizure, and ended up back in hospital. What a shit year it has been!

It's quite a family gathering in my room now, and then I am shocked to see Matty walking towards the bed with a big as grin on his face. He flew in today as a surprise. It's a bloody good surprise.

'Hi everyone,' I say slowly.

There are hugs and kisses and Matty makes some wisecrack. He's good at that. Distracting us from uncomfortable situations, but then he leans in for a hug and quietly says, 'Hi Bro. Love ya, mate.'

I am so happy to see them all, but especially Archie. How I love my little nephew. He is a bundle of love, with boundless energy and such an enquiring mind.

What's that Uncle Critter? What's that on your head? What is that button for? Why is there a tube in you? Does your bed go up and down? Have you got chocolate? What's in that bag?

Oh the energy of a three-year-old!

He is wearing a pirate-themed t-shirt and he says in his sweet, little bit lispy voice, 'When you are better Uncle Critter can we go to the park? Can we play on the pirate ship? I love pirates. Next birthday I will have a pirate party and we can wear eye patches and say AARRGGHH!'

'Yep, buddy, sounds good.'

I see the looks on their faces. Love tinged with concern. This year has been a hard journey for all of them.

It makes me remember how much love and support I have been shown by this family of mine and my friends. They have been here every step of this journey. Now that I am not allowed to drive anymore, I have had to rely on others to drive me to appointments, meals out, nights out, to the cricket, the footy, fishing and just hanging out. They have laughed with me, cried with me, scolded me and propped me up when I felt I couldn't manage alone. Yep, I am so loved.

As we talk about everything other than 'you know what' and my ears absorb the sounds of family chatting, I glance at my phone and am surprised to see that it is almost 5pm. It's been a good day and now the morning art show does not seem to have been so very long ago. But I'm exhausted. I can feel myself slipping.

My eyes are heavy. The words of my visiting family are becoming more distant.

'Hey bro.' It is Matty. 'Are you in pain?'

'Yeah, I think I need to sleep.'

'We'll take off and come back tonight. Okay?' he asks.

'That would be good, man,' I reply.

The next few minutes are filled with hugs and kisses and words of love. Archie climbs onto the bed with me and just lies there for a moment. I ask Mum to take a photo of us on my phone.

It is beautiful and I feel my heart full of love. Then they are gone, and I am left in a darkened room, alone. The sun is now just a lazy glow sitting in my window. The room is mellow, like warm honey dripping from a piece of freshly toasted bread. I am feeling reflective.

I saw Dad a couple of days ago, before he left to go back interstate for work. He told me he is going to hand in his resignation so he is around to do things with me. He asked me if there was any travelling I might want to do, and he could maybe come too. I think it's so he can make sure I am okay, but he says it like he thinks maybe it would be good buddy time!

I told him that the brothers and I talked about us going to Everest Base Camp, maybe he wants to come too? 'Maybe,' he said quietly.

Russ, my other brother, was over about a week ago for an early birthday party for Archie and will meet us all at Phillip Island for an early family Christmas in a few weeks time. It will be awesome to have us all together at our uncle's house on 'The Island'. I have such great memories of going there and hanging out with my cousins, Tom and Jack, when we were younger. Our parents would be having drinks and chatting and we boys would be outside playing cricket or chasey or just goofing off. I am determined to be well enough to get to Phillip Island for our family Christmas.

Another shift has started and a nurse I haven't seen before comes in to do my obs. She smiles and says, 'Hi Chris, I'm Kathy. Out of ten what is your pain level?'

'About an eight, I guess.'

She checks my chart, looks at the clock and says that I am due for some pain relief.

'I wouldn't say no to some help,' I reply.

The dinner trolley arrives while Kathy is busy checking my

temperature, which is a bit elevated, and my blood pressure which is still low, but within an acceptable range.

I can't face food at the moment, so let the lady delivering it put it on the tray at the foot of my bed and then she goes. Meanwhile, Kathy is fussing with my head bandage to check it's not too tight.

'Let's get some pain relief in,' she says.

After she leaves, I settle back and wait for the blessed relief. I hear voices outside my door as Kathy leaves and hear her say, 'Not too long, he has just had some medication for the pain and he needs to rest.'

My door opens slowly and around the doorframe I see the smiling faces of three good friends; Addaz, Trippa and Steph.

'Gidday, Critter,' says Addaz.

They come in with soft voices and loving hearts. They crowd around my bed and notice the untouched dinner tray at the end of my bed.

'Wow, Critter, you must be really crook. There's still food left,' quips Trippa.

Usually my appetite is legendary, but now ...

'Not that hungry, mate,' I reply.

We laugh and talk like close mates do, but all too soon I have fallen quiet, lost in my pain relief. I am drifting again. Wanting to succumb to solitude and peace.

'We should let you rest, mate,' they say.

'We'll call you tomorrow to see if you are up for a chat or a longer visit.'

These are good mates with lots of shared adventures. I am suddenly overwhelmed with nostalgia. The life I had, the life I should be living now. It's almost suffocating to think on it.

'Later, guys,' I say, as they bend over me to hug me and a smile, laden with sadness, sits on my mouth. It feels like a goodbye. Why? I wonder.

Alone. My room is dark and I don't want to reach for the bed lamp. I feel cocooned in a space of gentle warmth. I am not in pain now. I feel a reverie come over me. I lie back on my pillows and close my eyes.

Memories

Unsolicited snapshots of my life begin to play in my mind, like a movie. Times when I was very young and I was watching my family as they went about their lives. I was too small to speak but I could understand them. How, I now wonder, do I have a memory of watching them from my cot? That doesn't seem possible. And yet I can now clearly remember the day of my birth!

Everything looked hazy, viewed through a veil of mist. There were movements and shadows. Sounds that were unfamiliar and muffled.

I was lying immobilised, swaddled in something warm and soft. Gradually my eyes began to see images around me.

There were four figures of various heights. They were peering at me full of wonder. Their faces were beaming. They appeared to be VERY interested in me and I liked that! Then the sounds they had been making moved from gibberish to comprehension in my mind.

Oh, look at his full head of long black hair

Oh, look at his beautiful blue eyes

Oh, look at his barrel chest

AND OH!! Look at the size of that BIG TOE!!

Is it a good thing to have a BIG big toe on Planet Earth? I wonder why I said Planet Earth. How would I know that?

I wanted to ask these people standing above me, but when I opened my mouth to speak, a dreadful sound emerged; a wailing screech and water sprang from my eyes!

'What the heck, what is this?'

The people made cooing and shushing sounds and said, 'There, there, Darling.'

Then the man, who I now know as my dad, lifted me up carefully and held me close to his heart, all the while saying, 'There, there little boy, you are okay,' and as he unwrapped me from my restricted fabric, a wisp of cool air danced over my body.

It was then that I noticed that, whilst I might have had a huge big toe, I had a teeny, tiny body! 'Oh,' I thought, 'I wonder when I will get my BIG body. I had better look into that!' (So, of course I did and now I am taller and far more ripped than my brothers! Oh, did I also say more handsome too!)

Then my dad placed me on my mother's chest and instantly the warmth of her skin and the sound of her voice soothed and comforted me. The wailing screech stopped and the eye water disappeared. I felt safe and warm.

My family, who were instantly besotted with me (clearly!), gave me the name Christopher. My brother, Russ, at twenty-months-old had trouble saying that, so he said 'Critter,' and everyone laughed. And the nickname stuck.

I smile at that now. Right to this very moment, family and friends still call me Critter.

It is amazing to me that lying in this hospital bed now, I can recall with great clarity my first breath. I am reliving that first moment of feeling my beating heart. As I ponder that, I feel my heart beat a bit faster and I am caught in a memory so vivid, it literally takes my breath away. I am overwhelmed. What had I just experienced? I try to relax and my breath slows, and my heartbeat returns to normal. Post-operative reaction I wonder?

The memories return.

I remember that trying to understand the two phases of Earth were a mystery to me. A daytime, sun-filled and light and a night time, moon-filled and dark.

Learning to live in this two-phase world took some getting used to!

My parents groaned and 'tut tutted' when in the moon phase time I wanted to be wakeful and interminably hungry and in the sun phase, only napped distractedly, because I was still hungry. Some would say this has been the same all my life!

Eventually though, the rhythm of life began to make sense and my family and I all managed to settle into a pattern.

At first I could not speak their language but learnt soon enough that different sounds, facial expressions and eye water delivered to me all my needs.

I got to know them. A mum and dad and two brothers. We were a family. They all fussed over me, but my brother, Russ, would stare at me through the slats of my cot with a knowing look. Assessing the competition maybe? Still, as I got older and bigger, we were pretty much inseparable. That's not to say we didn't fight – boy did we fight – but we knew we had each other's backs, no matter what. The same with Matty who was seven years old when I arrived, he was the protector. Always helping to nurse me to sleep, bath me or cuddle me. He was always hovering, making sure I was okay. Like with Russ, over the growing up years we had many fights, some pretty hectic, but we always found our way back to one another. My connection to my brothers is really solid. Mum has always said to us boys, 'No one will ever love you like your brothers.' I reckon she is right and that's why causing them and the rest of the family so much concern weighs heavily on my mind.

As I ponder this, another memory muscles its way into my mind.

I am five, and we have all moved for Dad's work. We are living in New Zealand, in a town called Waihi, and I am running wild with my brothers on the ten acres that surrounded our house, chasing Jake our Rottweiler and Huey the Labrador and building a three-storey treehouse from rusty pieces of corrugated iron and offcuts of timber. That tree had about 300 nails in it! It was wobbly and dangerous, but Russ and I loved clambering about in it. We even made a rope swing attached to one of the branches. Russ fell from that tree and broke his arm one day, but as soon as he healed, we were back playing in it. We had a small motorbike and used to thrash around the property. Matty was at boarding school but came home every three weeks. We would wrestle and rumble and go exploring the abandoned mine shafts at the edges of the property. Apparently the signs saying, DO NOT ENTER! DANGER! were just for show! We all played Rugby Union because not to would have been a crime in New Zealand! The beach was nearby so we swam and surfed and climbed the headlands. It was awesome.

The scene changes again, and now I am ten and we are living in a mining town called Warrego, 53 kms from Tennant Creek in the Northern Territory, back in Australia. It is a harsh but beautiful landscape and, as the mine is closing down, the population is declining. Matty, my oldest brother, stayed in New Zealand at boarding school and Mum, Dad, Russ and I are living in Warrego. Eventually, Russ went away to boarding school in Alice Springs and, as the mine closed and more families left, I was the only non-indigenous kid at the Warrego Primary School. My teachers are an ex-Army officer and his wife; Mr and Mrs Baker, but sometimes we call them The Colonel and Mrs Colonel.

They are great and bring their two horses, Sadu and Hake, over from Armidale in NSW and teach me and the indigenous kids how to ride. We are taught Western style but also Stockman style by one of the indigenous men called Freddy Eight-Fingers (lost two roping cattle!). Horse riding is now part of our school curriculum. I ride during school time with the kids, before they are driven by Mr Baker back to their community about 30kms away. Sometimes I go in the troop carrier with the kids back to their camp. When we get back to Warrego, The Colonel and I take the horses out for a ride, come back and water them down, brush them, feed them and get them settled in for the night. The other great school subject The Colonel has introduced is swimming. Warrego has a great pool and with almost all the families gone now, it's just us and the kids who use it. Mr Baker says swimming is good for the indigenous kids' sinuses and eyes. Most of them can't swim at first, but soon we are good enough to join the Tennant Creek Competitions on a Friday night. We all load into the Troop Carrier and Mum and Dad's car and go in to swim against the town kids. At first they thought we

were just a joke, but after a while we started winning, and boy were they surprised!

I loved my time in Warrego. Being the only non-indigenous kid was so different to me. But the mob accepted me and even gave me my skin name, Tjangala. That was really special! It was a harsh landscape and very isolated, but I loved it. I remember I was sad when Dad said the town was finally being shut down. There were only seven of us left. Mum, Dad, Russ and I moved to Adelaide, and Matty followed twelve months later. We were finally all back together again.

Adelaide was a real shock after the isolation and freedom of Warrego. I recall starting high school at Pulteney Grammar and feeling very unsettled wearing a uniform and shoes every day! I guess it's fair to say that high school and I took a while to find a balance. I did eventually get into the rhythm of school and played sport and did my school work, reluctantly, but efficiently. I was just always so easily bored. I just wanted to get out and about and be doing things with my mates.

I smile. I still have good friends from my school years and then from the Old Scholars Football Club. I played for them after leaving school, until this year. Last year I co-captained the A grade. One of my proudest memories. Earlier this year, though, everything changed. I can't play footy any more, ever. I would love to pull on my **number 19** guernsey just one more time and have a run with the boys.

Still, our motto is **Once a Navy Blue, Always a Navy Blue ...** and that's bloody true!

It's like the slideshow has sped up. I see girlfriends and the times we shared. I remember when I first moved out of home. I am **nineteen** and move overseas with my girlfriend. My brother Matty is already living in London, so we stay with him for a bit, then get our own place. The great thing about living in London is that everything travel-wise is so accessible. We travel to Europe and do other trips but one of the highlights, is when we go to Oktoberfest in Munich for my twenty-first birthday. Russ flies over from Oz too! What a great birthday!

When I moved back to Oz **nineteen** months later, I moved back in with Mum and Dad. How hard was that!

This nostalgia is distracting me from a growing sense of unease that has been building for the last couple of days. It's not fear, more like an expectation of something about to change.

I guess it's because in about twenty hours we are meeting with my surgeon to get my results. She is amazing and I love that she always answers my questions with honesty and compassion. She is tiny and I have to bend down a long way to hug her. I know I am safe in her hands and I trust her, luckily, because she has handled my brain. Thinking on our next appointment I am aware that I don't want to dwell on it too much. It's emotionally too hard. The outcome possibilities are not all that fabulous, but what is that expression? 'Hope for the best and prepare for the worst.'

I look at the book where I wrote down my wish list. There is a lot more to add, but in this moment, in the depths of my heart, I know there is a change coming, and I might not be doing any of them.

Materna

'I have called for you because it's time for you to help one of your humans to exit. This one has been different, so your task will be more difficult.'

'Who?'

'It's the one you call Critter.'

The Evo messenger smiles a broad and dazzling smile. 'Has he managed to fulfil his Life's Mission already?'

'Well, yes, but it's a bit more complicated. He went to Earth by mistake.'

'What? Really? How is that possible?' the messenger asks.

'Well, it usually isn't, but in this one case there was, well, let's say, a mishap and he left as Ø19 to Earth, with no exit date and no life plan.'

'Oh goodness! So, what were the consequences of the error? He was supposed to be which number and go where?'

'He was originally assigned the destination of Ø16 and a life of solitude and learning. It was deemed that would settle his restlessness and teach him patience and stillness. Instead, the original Ø19 took that place. We have never navigated the likes of this before so I have watched them both very closely. Whilst the one known as Critter had to struggle to find his way, the original Ø19 we now know has thrived in that life of study and learning. He has been able to apply himself to the great texts and has embraced his Life's Mission. I wonder if he would have been as effective on Earth. Strangely, the one known as Critter has shown a courage and will that has actually helped him navigate the complexities of being human. It was an unexpected outcome for me to see that his heart truly was the catalyst for every decision he made. When he left for his mission, I said to him at the Celestial Slide that his heart held the key to his human experience. I knew how true that statement would be in the complexities of being human, but I was amazed to see how deeply he embraced the heart connection. At times it created great pain for him, but mostly great joy. Still, he managed to get on with life as a human and it's fair to say he has thrown himself into as many experiences as possible. He sometimes felt lost and directionless, but always managed to find his way. His stubbornness and energy have been invaluable. He has been a very busy human!'

The messenger is quiet and looks contemplative. 'How old is he in earth years?'

'Twenty six.'

'Oh, that's very young for a human to pass. I remember being human and even though I was old when it was my turn to exit, I recall the human desire to live, to have just one more day. Does he know yet? Has he begun to remember Ørtus?'

'He has started to reminisce and query why he can now recall things from his earliest days. He had a moment of recall when he touched his pregnant sister-in-law's belly and felt the new Evo assigned to that family, moving. He found the experience profound, and he hasn't realised yet that, in that touch, he left a small mark on the Evo's face, so when that little one is born, as a human boy, he will carry the mark as a memory of the one called Critter. This, of course, is not known by any of them yet.'

'He is starting to become reflective and contemplative. He doesn't know why, and his great realisation is about to unfold about his Life's Mission. That is why I have called for you. It's time to go to him, to assist him. I am sending you because you shared an affinity with him. He will be resistant to accept all the information you are going to impart. Be prepared to be challenged!'

'That's okay. I remember his personality and his determination. I think I will be able to bring him home. It's unexpected though, because I thought you were sending me to exit Lorna, my Earth wife', the messenger replied.

'No, that one has a strength and determination that has filtered down to her children, grandchildren and great grandchildren. She has not completed her Life's Mission yet, there are still wisdoms to dispense and challenges to meet with grace and patience. Her family are saddened by her illness, they call it dementia. They are angry that she is losing parts of her memory. Humans do not yet understand that what they fear, dementia, is just their loved one being "between the worlds." Still tenuously and deliberately attached to the mortal world because it is not their time to exit, but their spiritual self has begun the journey back to Ørtus – back home. She cannot hold onto all her Earthly memories, as she is inundated with her memories of Ørtus. It takes up all her time, all her dreaming. Her blue, blue eyes are becoming paler, preparing to come back into the luminous light of Ørtus. It won't be long until she is called home, and when that time comes, you can go and take the one they call Critter with you to help her exit.'

Critter

Whilst I have been lost in my memories, I have been very aware that there is still a place to go that I have been avoiding. Not a long, music-filled drive to explore this beautiful country, or a plane trip to an exotic destination. For this one, I need to be still. I need to be alone and I don't like being alone.

It's time, I know, to reach into my memory and tease at a thread that I have left until last. A most cherished one. One that has wound itself tightly around my heart and mind, tugging, calling me to visit.

I pull on the single strand and cautiously follow where it leads me. I already know where it's going, so I take a deep breath and tread gently into that memory.

Waiting in that quiet place in my heart is a girl, with sun-kissed skin, golden hair, an infectious laugh and a dazzling smile. Hannah. Her eyes tell me our story. For over four years we shared great adventures, and she filled my world. She taught me what true love is and I gorged in that joy. We were reckless and young. Eventually though, I was either too naïve or unaware to understand the full implications and responsibilities of true love. I can only wonder because, eventually, she also taught me that love also asks you to be who you are, authentically. With that in mind, she made her decision. I learnt what love isn't and in that day of breathtaking, heart-aching honesty, I realised that while she was now lost to me, she had found herself.

Letting go doesn't mean not loving someone. Perhaps it's the antithesis of that.

As I sit in that memory, I begin to experience an understanding so ridiculously simple that I am ashamed I have not seen it before now. I have this powerful moment of clarity. I am twenty six and, in my life, have been shown what absolute love looks like. Firstly from my family, then friends, and lovers. I have been surrounded by all forms of love, all my life.

I understand that it is the key to happiness and sadness. It can fill you or empty you. It emboldens you or makes you cower, but LOVE will always be the great teacher in our mortal life. And whilst I have received it from others, I know that I too have offered love, in all its incarnations to others.

I want to share this epiphany. This is important. There is ONLY love. Everything else is a distraction. Everything else is ego and façade. Love is our guide and our gentle master. Love is our now and our destiny. It is the past, the present and the future.

I feel giddy with excitement and I don't quite understand why this all seems so profoundly important to me. There is a feeling of urgency. Why?

My reverie is disturbed by the darkness of my room being lit up by the glow from my ringing phone. It's Mum.

'Hullo darling, I hope I didn't wake you. We were all thinking of coming in for a short visit, would that be okay?'

I want to interrupt her and tell her about my thoughts on love, but something stops me. I realise that I want to hold onto this thought a bit longer, just for me. I will share it tomorrow.

'Honestly, Mum, I feel pretty exhausted. It's um, let me see, okay, its 6.50pm now, it will be about 7.30pm before you get here, what if you all come back tomorrow after I hopefully get a decent night's sleep. I would love to see you, but …'

'It's okay,' she interrupts. 'Your rest is more important. We can come in the morning. I will text first. Would that be better?'

'Sounds good. Thanks Mum. Give my love to everyone there. I want to share something with you all tomorrow I have been thinking about, it's pretty weird, but I … Oh wait Mum, my nurse Kathy is here, hang on, I will call you back. Love you, bye.'

'Okay,' she says, 'talk soon. Love you.'

I meant to call Mum back as soon as the night nurse left, but I got distracted with some text messages from friends. I will call her in the morning.

Eventually, I allow myself to get caught by the exhaustion that has been chasing me all day. I succumb to sleep, blissfully, fully. I am now in a deep and wonderful sleep!

There is a tremendous roar and a pounding echoes in my head, but it's not a headache, it's something else! I hear the sound of a stormy wind flapping canvas sails.

I am the captain of a pirate ship!

A black cloth patch covers one of my eyes and I am steering a great wooden ship with authority. No driver's licence needed! Waves are lashing the deck and the crew is scurrying about. I recognise the crew, hundreds of them! They are my brothers, female and male friends and my footy mates. How can they all fit on the ship? This is AWESOME! The storm is getting fiercer and the ship is lurching dangerously from side to side.

'We'll head for Pirie Cove, right through the Saracens Heads,' I roar above the howl of the storm. 'Once docked, we will only be a Stone's Throw from the Lady Grace Tavern. We will wait out the storm with Old Mates, good food, wine and wenches!'

'Aye Aye Cap'n!' they shout.

Oh, the FREEDOM!

Life full and filled with adventure! I am strong and fit and completely invincible. What a feeling!

It's so real. I touch my face, expecting to feel an eye patch, moist from the ocean spray. I think I will have to unfurl one of my hands that are knotted and cramping from clutching a ship's wheel, holding it steady, as I struggle against the building storm. Instead, I feel a nose tube and something stuck into the back of my hand. My tongue darts around tasting sea salt on my lips, but I then realise it's actually tears. My tears.

The room is very dark and there are no sounds from the outside corridor. I struggle to focus my eyes through the tears and then see the room with clarity. Not a pirate ship, just a hospital bed. Then, something else. An ache in my heart and knowing that things are about to change. The pain in my head is back, and tears drop onto my hospital gown. I am not crying because of the pain, but for the months of fear and sadness that I have fought to keep at bay. I weep for all those who love me and who look at me with their hope and their own fear.

I fumble around in the darkness for the tissue box to wipe the tears from my eyes, and then I blink, hard. The pain is momentarily forgotten!

'Pop?' I whisper. More vigorous eye rubbing.

'Pop?' I say again.

And so it is. My pop is standing by my bed, dressed in his fishing shorts, t-shirt and cap. Pop, all barrel chested and bandy legged, places one of his massive hands on my shoulder and I spy the gold onyx ring on his little finger.

'You've been doing it tough, old mate,' he says.

I am dumfounded. I want to laugh, to cry, I want to hug my pop.

'How can you be here, you're ... um ... you know ... GONE. About six months ago.'

He smiles and I see the gold-capped front tooth and the creases around his eyes. He looks deeply into my face and then says, 'I know it's a bit hard to understand, buddy, but I will try my best.'

'Wait,' I interrupt. 'I must be hallucinating. I went to your funeral, Pop. It was a bloody dreadful day and the storms were epic. Half of Sydney was blacked out and we all laughed and joked that it was caused by you, so all the electricians, like you were, could get heaps of overtime! But it was also so sad. We all thought you were invincible!'

But wait, why am I having a conversation with my hallucination?

'Pop, this can't be real. Am I losing my mind? Is this from the surgery? Am I ...'

'Whoa, buddy, take a breath. I know it's overwhelming, but do you trust me?' he asks. 'I did die and I have seen how this all works. I am here to explain part of what's going on with you.'

I STILL cannot believe my eyes or ears, but hey, this dream or hallucination I am having has taken away my exhaustion and has provided me with some much-needed entertainment, so what have I got to lose?

'Okay, Pop, I am all eyes and ears, bring it on.'

I say it with a voice that sounds playful, and maybe a bit smug. After all, it's just me and my hallucination chatting! My Pop died six months ago after a short illness. He had always been fit, strong and independent. He looked after my gran for many years after she developed Parkinson's and dementia, and it broke his heart when he couldn't look after her anymore. She has been in a nursing home now for about eight years and, until about a couple of months before he died, Pop visited her every day.

Pop and I received our crap diagnoses in the same week. Him in Sydney, being told he had lung cancer from being exposed to asbestos as a young apprentice electrician at Cockatoo Docks in the 1940s, and me in Adelaide being told—

'Critter!' the Pop imposter interrupts my thoughts, 'are you ready? This is going to be some surprise.'

'Sure,' I say.

'The process has been in existence from the beginning, and the beginning was infinite eons ago. This is your story ...'

***

The room has become completely black and silent. I cannot hear the sounds of the ward outside or the monitors next to my bed. There is not a speck of light. It is the darkest dark and yet I feel calm. I can't see the Pop figure, but feel his hand on my shoulder.

I am completely at peace. A peace I have never experienced before.

He starts to tell me the most fantastic tale and in one part suggests that one of the 'Evos' had caused a ripple in the system, and with that came uncertainty and the potential for disruption to the order of Ørtus.

He looks very intently at me when he says this!

When he finishes speaking, I lie in stunned silence, eyes firmly shut. This is all too fantastic, too impossible to absorb. What have I just heard? I used to be a being called an Evo on a heavenly world called Ørtus. There, a Universal mother called Materna looked after us. I was supposed to be assigned the life of Ø16, but due to a mishap, I was sent to Ø19's life, to Earth, where I always wanted to go. I wasn't given my Life's Mission to complete and not told my exit date and now my Pop is here to set me right.

What nonsense is this?

Perhaps my surgery has damaged some part of my brain, so now I am imagining my dead Pop and dreaming of fantastical lands in far-off galaxies. Maybe that and the pain relief have made me delirious!

But wait! What if this is all true?

'Is it my time to die?' I ask.

As these words escape my mouth I feel the full weight of their meaning. I am 26-years-old with an unacceptable medical diagnosis, but I have HOPE that within the next few years there will be a cure or a trial I can be involved in that will offer better outcomes than what is currently available.

I look down at my arm and see the black and pink wristband that I have worn for the last ten months. It says **STRONG ENOUGH TO LIVE**. My dear friend Shelley found this saying and gave it to me: *You were given this life because you are strong enough to live it.*

She said, 'I thought of you, Chris, when I read this. You've got this!'

Now **SETL** has become my mantra and that of my family and friends. There are hundreds of these wristbands in the world now, reminding people that they are stronger than they might know.

'Am I going to die?' I ask again.

'Well, Critter, your exit date was destroyed in a mishap, all we got was '19'. Materna is the only one who knows for sure. As a result, you have a choice, and that's unheard of! I have been sent to tell you that you have completed your Life's Mission and done a bloody good job! So you can come back to Ørtus with me knowing that the time is right, or you can choose to stay. Materna thought that you may need some guidance, and she has selected me.'

'You talk about my Life's Mission, but what have I done? I haven't done anything extraordinary or memorable. I am only now ready to take my place in the world. I have finished my studies, I have a job and before I got sick I was thinking of travelling again. I haven't lived long enough to have DONE anything worthwhile yet.'

'Ah, Critter, humans always place so much importance on thinking that their legacy or efforts have to be grand and extraordinary. And for some who come to Planet Earth that is their role. But for many, it is the kindness you bring to the world by being the best version of yourself. Greatness is not necessarily measured by the tangible, but the intangible ways humans interact.

'In your case, Critter, you have faced your trials and tried to learn from them. You have certainly pushed the boundaries and explored every experience. It has been observed by Materna that you did many things the hard way, with difficult outcomes. But, in EVERY instance, you accepted the consequences of your decisions and behaviours and tried to do things differently. Your greatest legacy though, mate, is your overwhelming capacity for LOVE. Many have been loved by you and many have loved you in return. Your large heart has been full of love and has worked overtime to engage with as many people as possible. That heart of yours has certainly been tested.

'You may not realise the impact you have had on others. But I assure you, those who know and love you, will never forget you. Trust that their love for you and your wellbeing is greater than their pain of losing you.

'So, buddy, this is the part where you get to choose. Come back to Ørtus with me now because you have finished your Life's Mission or stay and face an uncertain future.'

'You mean, leave, lea— Go with YOU?' I stutter.

'Yes. Every human who passes is visited by a loved one who has gone before them, they are then assisted to make the transition and spend some time in another realm, like a halfway stop, before fully returning to Ørtus. In this halfway place, they are met by many of their passed-over loved ones who will assist in their transition from the Human to the Energy being. It's a wonderful time of great joy not connection.'

But if it WAS happening, how could I decide what to do? I think about my family, and see their faces in my mind's eye. They have each other. They love one another and would always be there for one another. They will be okay.

I think about my friends and I know that they will all go on and live full and wonderful lives with or without me. Bloody hell, most of them will become mums and dads, just like I want. But they will get to do all of that without me. Still, I will be there with them, just in a different way. I think of the golden-haired girl with the beautiful eyes and know that she will find the happiness and love she deserves.

I think of all the things on my wish list. If I leave now, I will certainly never achieve them. But staying won't guarantee it either.

My mind is racing. I recall a conversation with my beautiful surgeon who told me that if this latest biopsy shows another tumour, then my prognosis would be even more unsatisfactory. What to do?

'Pop, can you help me decide?'

'I can't advise you, Critter. I only have a few of your Earth hours here before I will be called back. I will go with or without you. It's your choice, mate.'

My mind is in a spin.

I am beginning to accept that this is not a dream or an hallucination. This is real. I am at the crossroads of my life. Now I understand the flashbacks and the memories of a place and time that seemed ethereal and yet familiar to me. I understand now why I have had the strange feeling that I won't achieve my wish list, why I have been feeling apprehensive. It's all becoming clear now. It isn't because of the impending results of my surgery, but because I literally have a Life or Death decision to make, and I have to make it now.

More images of my life scroll through my mind. Some are harder to watch than others. I can see that my life has been full and fast and filled with adventure. There have been glad times and sad times. I have been blessed to know great love and been brought to my knees with sadness and regret. And yet, through it all I always just wanted connection. I wanted love.

The faces of everyone I love rise before me, and instantly my decision is made. I know that they will understand that I loved them enough to leave them.

I have fully embraced this Earth life, but the memory of Ørtus is creeping gently into my consciousness. I can feel the warm, unconditional love of Materna, and the tranquillity and serenity of my previous home.

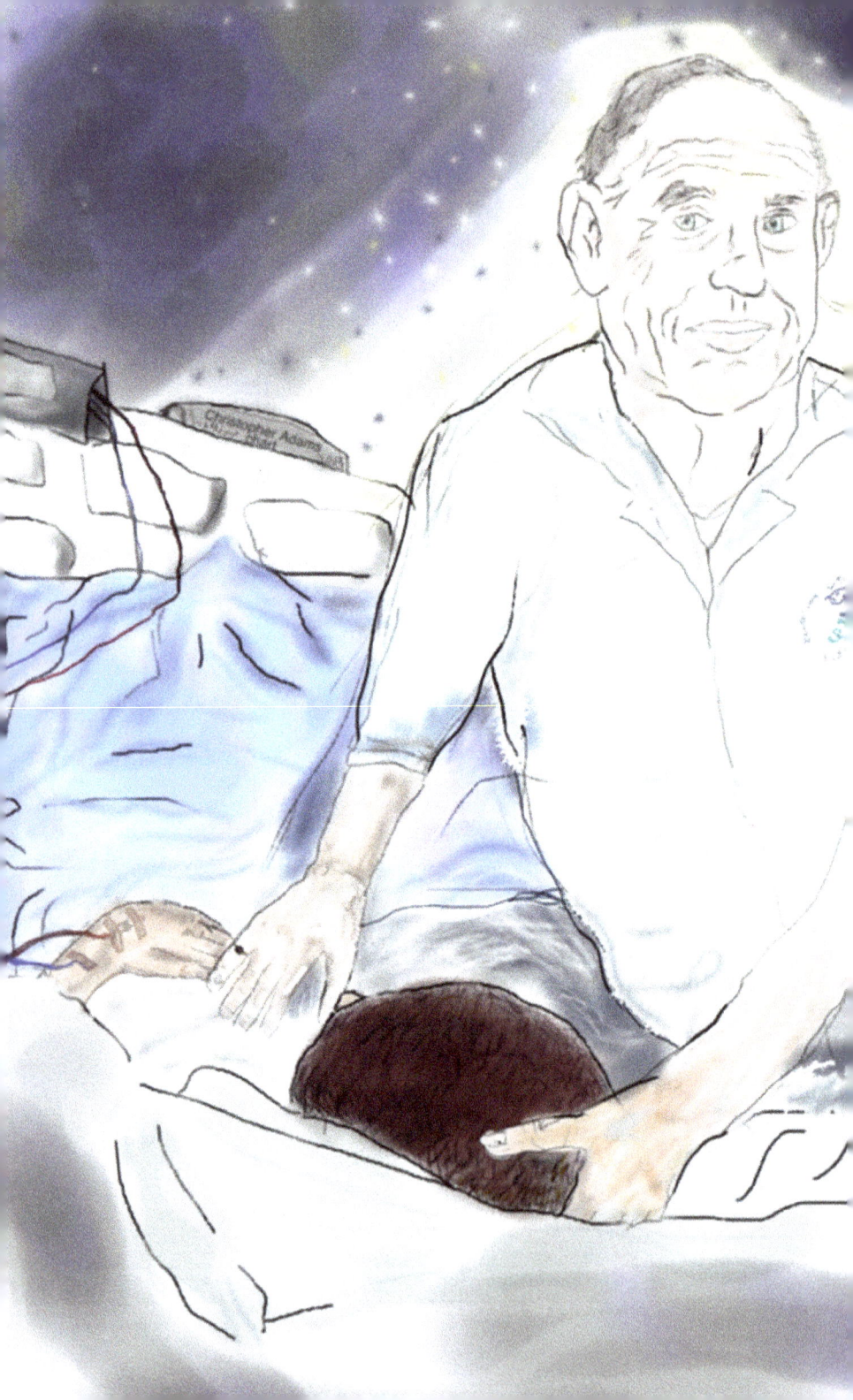

I finally understand why this Earth life had been so fast and furious. I had wanted Earth, and somehow got it! But with that came this journey, this ending. As I look at the clock on the wall opposite my bed, I note that it is 2.10 am and the date: 19 November, 2015. There is the number **19** again, the number that has featured so heavily in my life.

My heart begins to beat fast and loud. It knows. My heart has known that its job was to beat for **26 years, 54 days, 15 hours, 1 minute** and who knew how many seconds before its job was done. I am potentially seconds away from my last heartbeat.

I am not afraid. I am not sad. I am going home!

'I understand it all now, Pop. It's all so clear. All the experiences, all the challenges, the joy and the heartbreak. I know it was the life I was given, mistakenly, but it became mine and I LOVED IT!'

'It's my time. I'm ready. Take me home, Pop.'

Pop had one hand on Critter's shoulder and lifted his other large hand onto Critter's chest. In that instant, Critter saw before him all those he loved, and he smiled. Then, his love-filled, compassionate heart, gave one last almighty beat. The vibrations of that heartbeat travelled out into the world and nestled into the hearts of all those he loved while they slept or worked or played,

Then it stopped.

Going home

Everything changed!

Pop became much larger. Gone were the thongs, the bandy legs, the fishing shirt and hat, gone was the gold front tooth, the pinky finger onyx ring and the barrel chest. What was before my eyes now was an image of unimagined beauty. I was witnessing absolute and eternal love. Not a form, just glowing energy that emitted a slight hum, and a vibration that enveloped me.

I, too, no longer had human form. I was pure energy and light. I also had something like wings that were shimmering in the glowing energy that I now thought of as my body. They were made of light-filled, translucent shapes and were completely weightless.

I felt, rather than heard, how Pop communicated with me now.

You don't leave Planet Earth as you arrived, on a Celestial Slide, now you leave in this form and it's far more exciting!

I thought of my family and friends and knew with complete understanding that now I would be able to watch over them and keep them safe. I will love them unconditionally for all eternity.

But how will they know I am still with them? I wondered.

You can send them signs; they just have to be open to looking for them. Choose whatever you want, Pop said.

I looked at my new form and plucked one of the shimmering shapes. As it left the vibrating energy it turned into a grey-blue feather and I knew I had my answer. **Whenever they see a feather, of any colour, they will know I am close by …**

The feather floated away from my new being and settled on the now vacant hospital bed.

The Pop form communicated, *If you are ready, we can go now.*

An opening appeared in the drab green wall opposite the bed. I saw music, heard colours, felt a luminous light that embodied peace and unconditional love. It was mesmerising and oh so tranquil. I was being shown the universe where Ørtus sat and where I would eventually return.

I seemed to float through the opening and was immediately cradled in a space that felt like home. There were beings that held me and I knew they had been my ancestors and family from Earth life. There are only feelings of joy and peace. Feelings of belonging, of returning.

I am forever.

Epilogue

I see you.

You are wearing a bright orange top. Your earrings and lipstick match, of course! You stop in the doorway, looking confused. You step outside and check the room number. It's the right room. I see you screw up your face, puzzled.

There is something on the bed that catches your attention. You reach for it and find yourself holding a beautiful blue and grey feather. Your puzzled look sits a little longer, and then it changes. Now your face is still. You stand motionless and gaze at the 'doorway' in the wall through which I have floated, but there is nothing for you to see. Just a green painted wall, yet you stare at it intently.

A tear begins its journey on your eyelash rim, spills down your cheekbone, finds the hollow of your cheek, curves around your jawbone and then perches precariously off the end of your chin. It hovers there, waiting. Then as you blink and add more tears to the flow, it becomes full and bulbous and drops off your chin, free falling onto your chest. You gasp as it rests on your heart.

Love, unconditional and eternal resides within you.

'Critter,' you whisper …

Critter's wish list

1. Leave hospital and NEVER come back because I am 100% healthy!

2. Find the best PHO restaurant in Adelaide (or the world!) and order the biggest bowl ever.

3. Get back into the gym and be SO WELL, so recovered, that I would lift the heaviest weight and my great mate Jack would be envious and goggle-eyed with surprise!

4. Pull on my number 19 footy guernsey and play footy again with my beloved Navy Blues. Maybe I will take a specky mark, and then kick an impossible goal to clinch the Grand Final! (Well, Mum did say I could choose ANYTHING!)

5. Go to the animal shelter and choose a sweet-as dog. A lab or a boxer who I will call Boss. We will be inseparable.

6. Move out of home. Yeah, a place of my own with Boss where my friends can come over for frothies and a barbie.

7. Buy a new suit, shirt, tie, shoes and grab my favourite girl for a fabulous night out on the town. The best restaurant, clubs and dancing, not coming home till the sun comes up.

8. Travel overseas again. Maybe this time on a one way ticket and just see it ALL.

9. Oh, I need to get my licence back. Once my eyesight improves after all the surgeries.

10. Go on a road trip with Boss to the Kimberleys, camping under the Milky Way. Throw the fishing lines in the back.

11. Go to lots of music concerts with my brothers and mates, here and overseas.

12. Climb to Everest Base Camp with Matty and Russ like we planned, once I am well. How awesome will it be to stand, the three of us, on the top of the world!

13. Be the BEST uncle ever to Archie and to the new little boy due in February, and any more that might come along! 💗

14. Go to THE MCG with family and mates and watch Collingwood, the Mighty Magpies, win another Grand Final!

15. Buy a house with a big backyard for the kids and for friends.

16. Find the woman that I can give my complete heart and soul to.

17. Be a husband.

18. Be a dad myself!

19. Be the best ME I can be

20. LIVE LIFE FULLY.

About the Author

Cherrie Adams lives in Adelaide, South Australia, but was born in Sydney in the 1950s. She is married and has three sons, and two grandsons. Cherrie works as a Counsellor in her own business, Mrs Havachat Counselling. The catalyst for writing this book was the death of her youngest son, Christopher (Critter) in November 2015. Her musings on grief led to two pieces being published; one titled, *When Grief Came to Town* in an online contribution to Psychology Today, and the second, *Gang of Seven*, which featured in a collection of works from around the world in a book called *Fear and Courage*.

Writing became a way to process her grief and eventually led her to the thought of writing a book. She knew she didn't want to write a clinical story about her son's medical and emotional journey with brain cancer. The book took an unexpected turn when she realised that by reframing the actual events, she was able to offer her son the empowerment and choice that he had been deprived of by his disease. It became her final gift to him. In her book, Cherrie explores the concept of finding our way in life, returning home and trusting that we are 'strong enough to live the life we have been given'.

About the Illustrator

Lucinda Gregory is an Adelaide based, self-taught artist and illustrator. With a background in graphic design and cake design (patisserie), Lucinda immerses herself in many fields of creativity. Visual art and illustration are her favourite creative outlets, with photography holding a dear place in her heart and recently experimenting with lino print and pottery, she is a wearer of many hats. Lucinda's dreamy, ethereal abstract artwork is pleasing to the eye and enhances the viewers' imagination.

In 2015, Lucinda was diagnosed with a rare brain stem tumour, which consequently left her with chronic pain and disability. Since her miraculous lifesaving and life-changing surgery, Lucinda has re-taught herself how to paint and draw left-handed, as the tumour unfortunately took her right, dominant side. Lucinda is on the path to become a social worker, with a passion in working in mental health and wellbeing of brain injury and spinal cord injury patients. Lucinda is an ambassador for the Neurosurgical Research Foundation and continues to raise awareness of brain cancers.

Acknowledgments

Heartfelt thanks to my husband Martin, and my sons Matty and Russ for your love, and understanding how vital it was for me to write this story, my way. I have tried to honour your son and your brother whilst being mindful of your own grief journey.

To Jen and Ellie for being there for us all and offering your gentle support.

To my grandson Archie, nephew to Critter, who made his last months so full of love and laughter.

To Maxi who, even in utero, managed to connect with his uncle just a day before Critter left. He felt your lifeforce and, no doubt, your spirit.

To Hannah for the love and joy she brought to Critter's life.

To Lucinda for bravely accepting the challenge to provide the illustrations even though you were concerned about the outcomes. You need not have worried, they are wonderful.

To the beautiful Dr Amal Abou-Hamden who showed such love and care to Critter. You made a difference to his journey because of your skill, empathy and humanity.

To EVERYONE who shared Critter's or our lives, you have all had a role in this story. You know who you are and what you mean to us, and to him.

To the wonderful team at NRF who work tirelessly to find better outcomes for those who suffer from brain tumours, brain cancer and other neurological related disorders. Your work is vital.

To Blaise and Busybird Publishing for the hand holding and for riding my emotional rollercoaster with me. What started as a work relationship has become a much cherished friendship. You, Blaise, saw my vision more clearly than most and your unwavering support for me to write the story I needed to write gave me the confidence to tell this story.

SETL

Strong Enough To Live (SETL) was initiated by Critter. It is from the saying, *You were given this life because you are strong enough to live it.* Critter adopted it, not only as a mantra to guide him through his illness, but also as the catchphrase for his fundraising activities. Our family has carried on Critter's legacy and continues to raise funds under the Strong Enough To Live banner. It is also the name of a Facebook group that allows people to reflect on Critter's life and support the wider group of people who are affected by brain cancer. Strong Enough To Live remains a source of inspiration to all those who knew and loved Critter.

All proceeds from this book will be donated by Strong Enough to Live to the Adelaide-based Neurosurgical Research Foundation to fund brain cancer research. If you would like to support Strong Enough To Live, please email setl@aapt.net.au.

www.ingramcontent.com/pod-product-compliance
Lightning Source LLC
Chambersburg PA
CBHW040417100526
44588CB00022B/2852